**Editor**
Nancy Hoffman

**Managing Editor**
Karen Goldfluss M.S. Ed.

**Editor-in-Chief**
Sharon Coan, M.S. Ed.

**Cover Designers**
Charles Adler
Lesley Palmer

**Imaging**
Rosa C. See
Nancy Hoffman

**Product Manager**
Phil Garcia

**Trademarks**
*QuickTime* and the *QuickTime* Logo are trademarks used under license.

**Publishers**
Rachelle Cracchiolo, M.S. Ed.
Mary Dupuy Smith, M.S. Ed.

# MULTIMEDIA

## *Collections*

## WORLD WAR II

**Authors**

*Paul Gardner and Jamie Wu Liu*

***Teacher Created Materials, Inc.***
6421 Industry Way
Westminster, CA 92683
www.teachercreated.com
**ISBN-0-7439-3043-6**

# Table of Contents

# Introduction

The following guide is provided to assist teachers and students as they prepare to use the photographs, clip art, audio clips, video clips, and documents presented on the multimedia CD. The images and clips provide effective resources that teachers and students can use to enhance presentations and projects.

For your convenience, thumbnail images of the photos and clip art that appear on the multimedia CD are included at the end of this section. They can be viewed in advance to decide which images to use for a particular project or lesson. A list of the audio clips, documents, and video clips is also included.

Whether used for a student's written report or multimedia presentation, to enhance an instructional lesson, or to stimulate students' critical thinking, you will discover that the resource materials on the multimedia CD will help enrich your learning experiences.

## Technical Support

**Phone: 1-800-858-7339**

**Email: custserv@teachercreated.com**

**Web Address: http://www.teachercreated.com/support**


## Acknowledgments

*HyperStudio*® is a registered trademark of Knowledge Adventure.

*Print Shop*® is a registered trademark of Mattel Interactive.

# System Requirements

## Requirements for Macintosh

- 32 MB RAM
- PowerMac/100 MHz or faster
- System 8.0 or later
- Color Monitor (1000s colors)
- QuickTime 4.0 (or later)*
- 4X CD-ROM (or faster)

## Requirements for Windows

- 32 MB RAM
- 486/100 MHz or faster
- Windows 95/Windows 98
- Color Monitor (High Color-16 bit)
- QuickTime 4.0 (or later)*
- 4X CD-ROM (or faster)

******QuickTime*** is available on the CD-ROM or can be downloaded from: *http://www.apple.com/quicktime* See the ReadMe file for installation of *QuickTime* from the CD-ROM. Make sure you choose "Recommended" or "Full" as the installation type.**

 

## Getting Started

Since the program runs directly from the CD-ROM, there is nothing to install. However, if you use an older computer or have adequate disk space, it is recommended that you copy the entire CD-ROM onto your hard drive so that it will run more efficiently.

> ***Macintosh Users:*** In some cases, the viewer program will not work correctly with *Adobe Type Manager* installed on Macintosh. If you are unable to see media in the program, it is recommended that the **ATM** control panel be turned off. To do this, open the **Extensions Manager** in the **Control Panels** folder in the **Apple** menu. Uncheck the **ATM** control panel, save the settings, and restart the computer.

**Follow these instructions to run the program directly from the CD-ROM.**

*Macintosh Users*

1. Insert the CD-ROM into the drive.
2. When the CD icon appears on the desktop, double-click the CD-ROM to open it.
3. Double-click the Player icon to start the program (Figure 1).

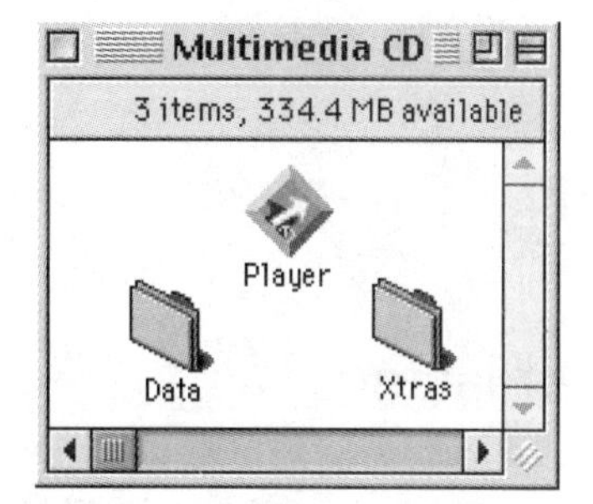

*Figure 1*

*Windows Users*

1. Insert the CD-ROM into the drive.
2. If the CD screen (Figure 1) does not appear, click on the Start menu and then the Run menu (Figure 2).
3. Click the Browse button and locate the CD-ROM.
4. Locate the Player.exe file and double-click to start the program.

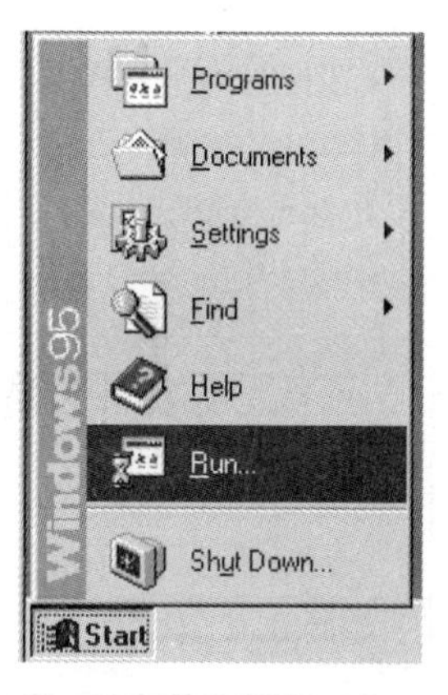

*Figure 2*

If you see a message that says "This program requires *QuickTime* version 4.0 or later...," you need to install *QuickTime*. Click on the QuickTime Installer on this CD-ROM, or download *QuickTime* from *http://www.apple.com/quicktime*

**Follow these instructions to copy the CD-ROM onto your hard drive and run the program from the hard drive.**

*Macintosh Users*

1. Drag the entire CD-ROM icon to your hard drive.
2. When the CD-ROM icon appears on your hard drive, double-click it to open the CD-ROM.
3. Double-click the Player icon to start the program.

*Windows Users*

1. Copy the contents of the CD-ROM into a folder on your hard drive.
2. Locate the Player.exe file and double-click to start the program.

# Using the Viewer Program

## The Main Menu

This is the menu that appears after the program is started.

**Desktop**
Click to return to the desktop.

**Audio Clips**
Click to browse only audio clips.

**Clip Art**
Click to browse only clip art.

**Documents**
Click to browse only documents.

**Photographs**
Click to browse only photographs.

**Video Clips**
Click to browse only video clips.

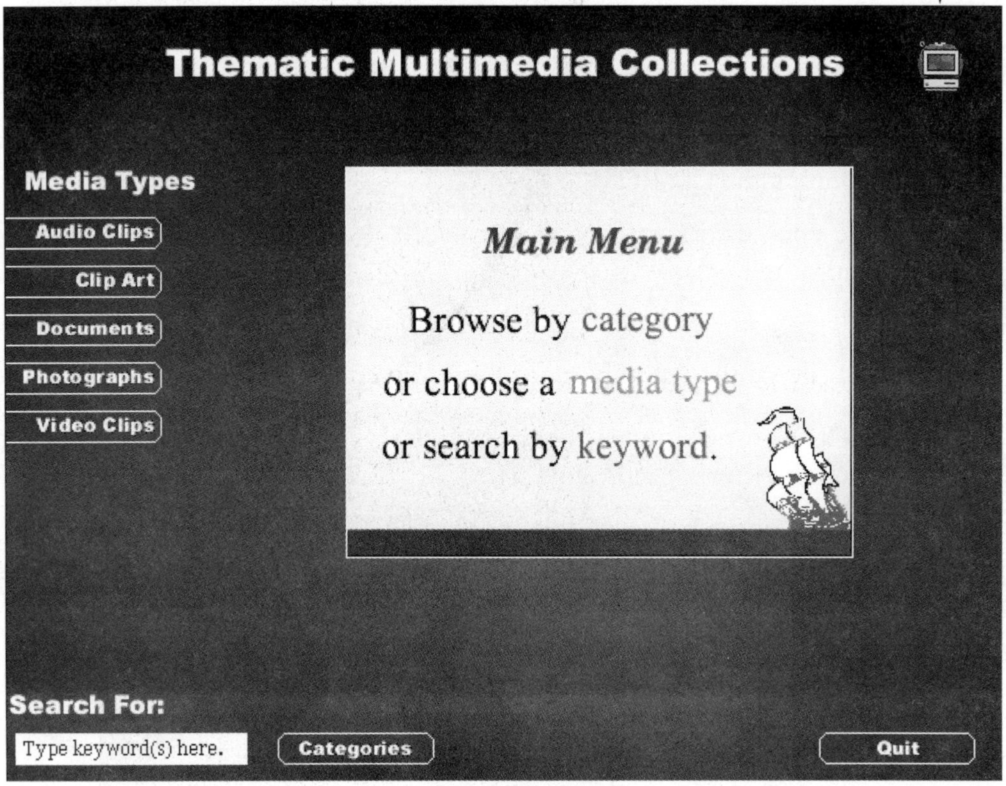

Thematic Multimedia Collections

Media Types

Audio Clips

Clip Art

Documents

Photographs

Video Clips

*Main Menu*

Browse by category

or choose a media type

or search by keyword.

Search For:

Type keyword(s) here.

Categories

Quit

**Search For:**
Type a keyword in the box and press Enter (Return) to search all media in the collection or the files in each media type.

**Categories**
Click to view the categories.

**Quit**
Click to quit the program.

## Using the Viewer Program

The viewer program provided on the multimedia CD allows the user to easily access the media by either browsing or searching with keywords. The user can choose a media type (audio clips, clip art, documents, photographs, or video clips) and browse the files in that media, or the user can choose a category and browse the files by categories. By entering a keyword(s) or the first few letters of a word, a search can be done to find specific files in all of the media types or in one particular media type.

### Browsing by Media Type

1. Click a media type button (**Audio Clips, Clip Art, Documents, Photographs,** or **Video Clips**) to view the list of files in that media type.

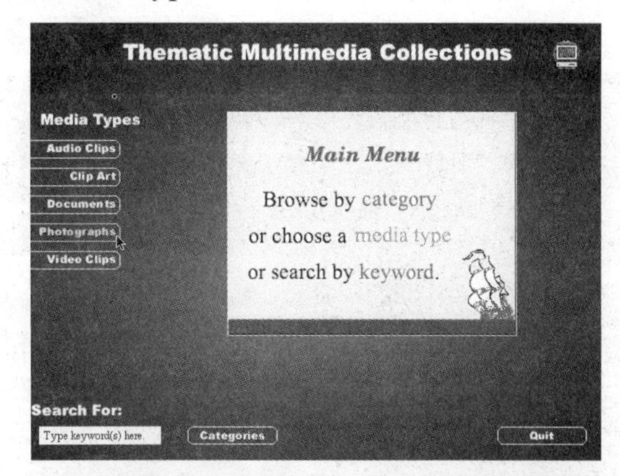


2. Click a file on the list to listen to the audio clip or look at the picture, document, or video clip.

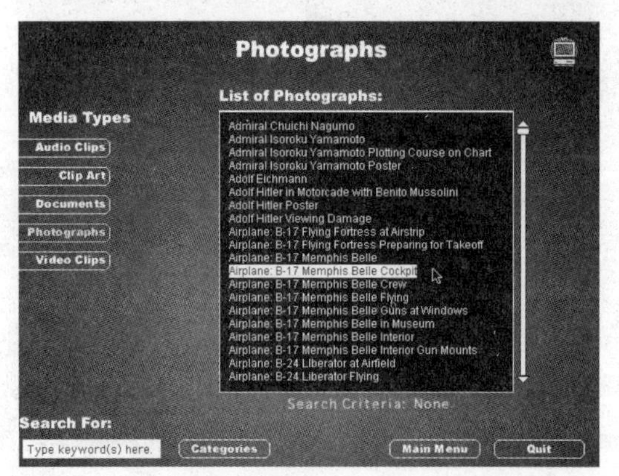


3. Click the **Back to List** button to return to the list. Click the **Right Arrow** to listen to the next audio clip or view the next picture, document, or video clip. Click the **Left Arrow** to go back to the previous item on the list.

## Searching by Keyword

The user can search in all media types.

1. Click on the **Main Menu** button to go to the main menu if you are not already there.

2. Type a keyword in the **Search For:** box and press **Enter (Return)** to view the list of search results. If no result is returned, try a different keyword. Typing in only the first few letters of a word gives the same result as when the entire word or a variation of this word is typed.

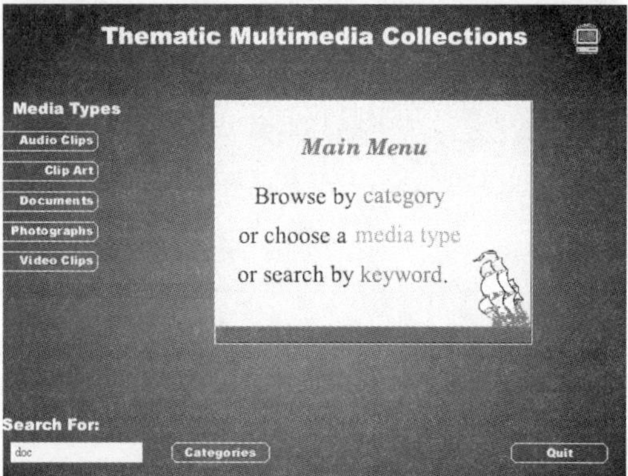


3. Click a file on the list to listen to the audio clip or look at the picture, document, or video clip.

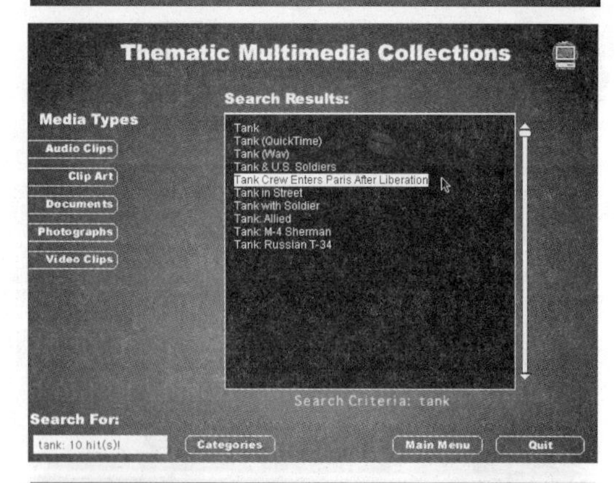


4. Click the **Back to List** button to return to the list. Click the **Right Arrow** to listen to the next audio clip or view the next picture, document, or video clip. Click the **Left Arrow** to go back to the previous item on the list.

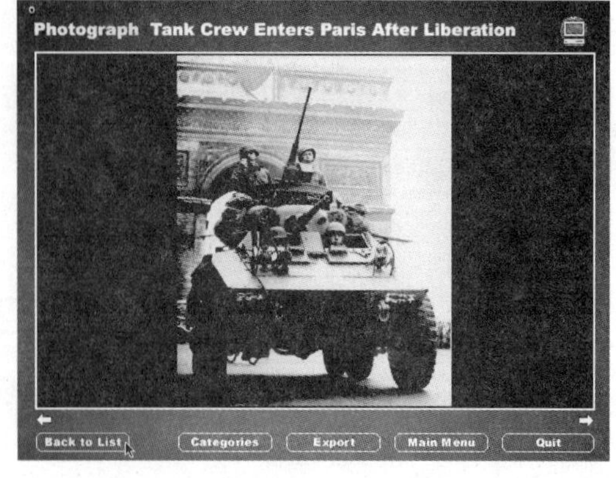


 

## Searching by Keyword *(cont.)*

The user can also search in each media type.

1. Click the **Audio Clips** button.

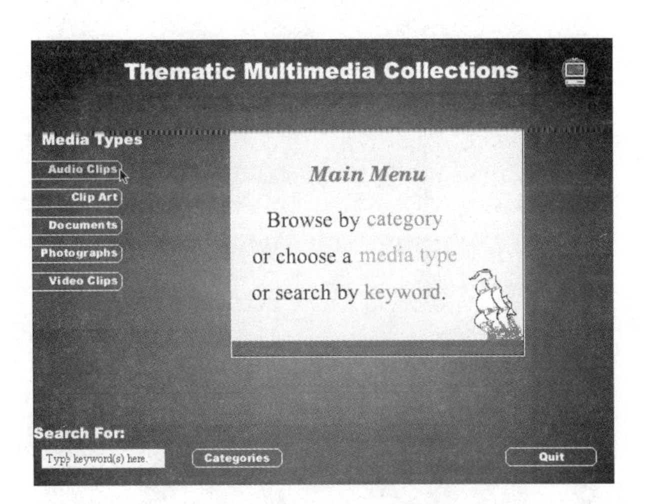

2. Type a keyword in the **Search For:** box and press **Enter (Return).**

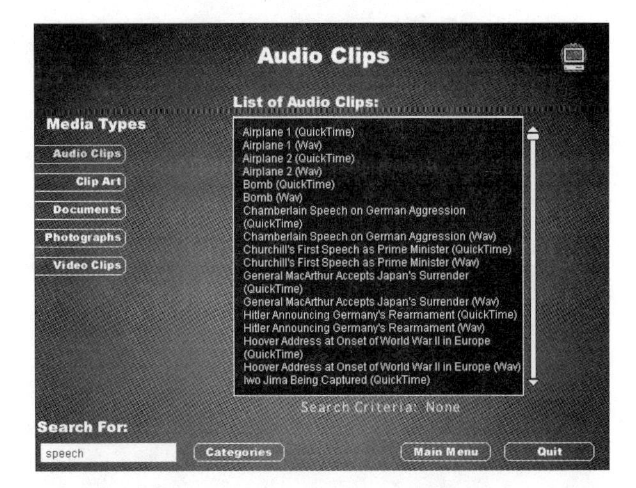

3. Click a file on the list of search results to select an audio clip (below left).
4. An audio control bar appears in the center of the screen (below right). Hold down the **Volume** key on the far left and scroll up or down to adjust the volume control. To listen to the audio clip, press the **Play** key (second from the left). Click on the **Rewind** key (second from the right) to rewind. The **Fast Forward** key is on the far right.

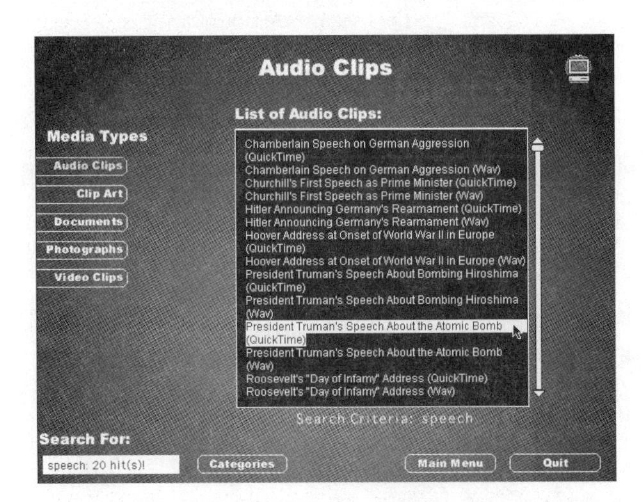

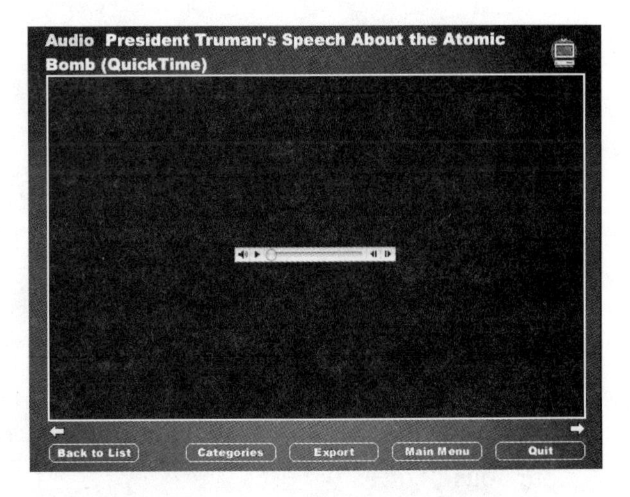

5. To search in another media type, click on the **Main Menu** button. Then, select that media type.

## Browsing by Category

1. Click the **Categories** button to view the list of categories.

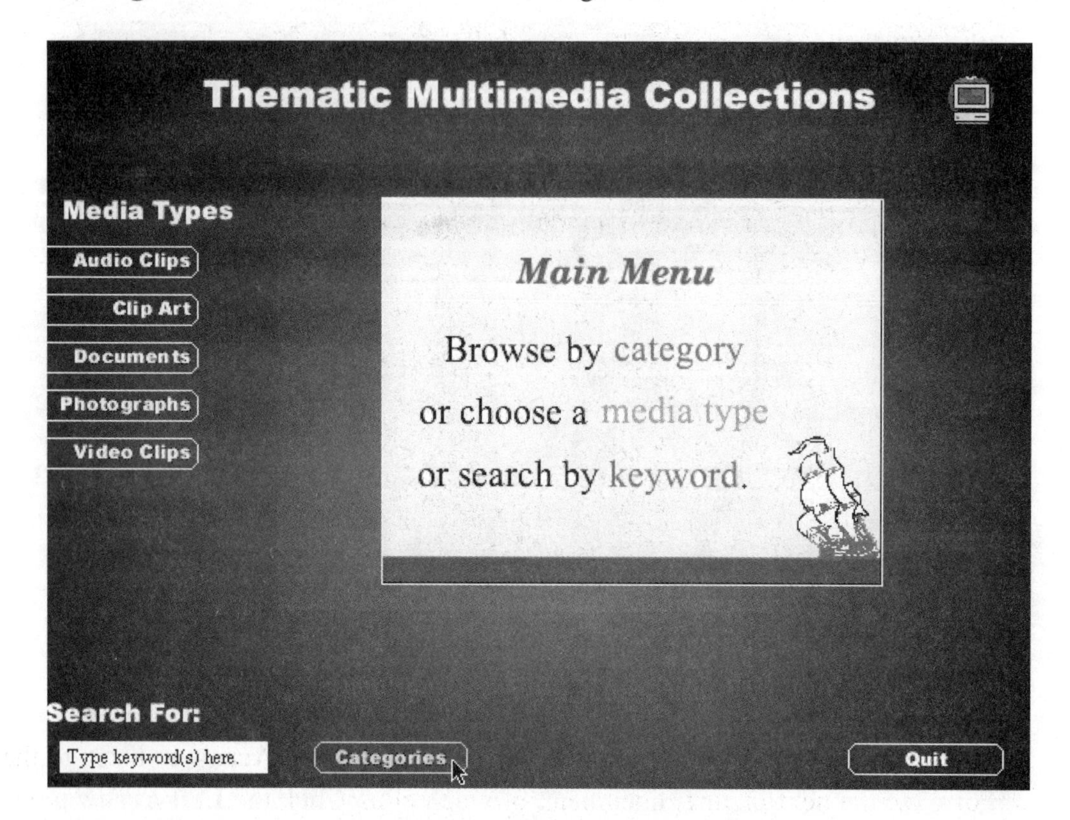


2. Click on a category title to view the files listed in that category.

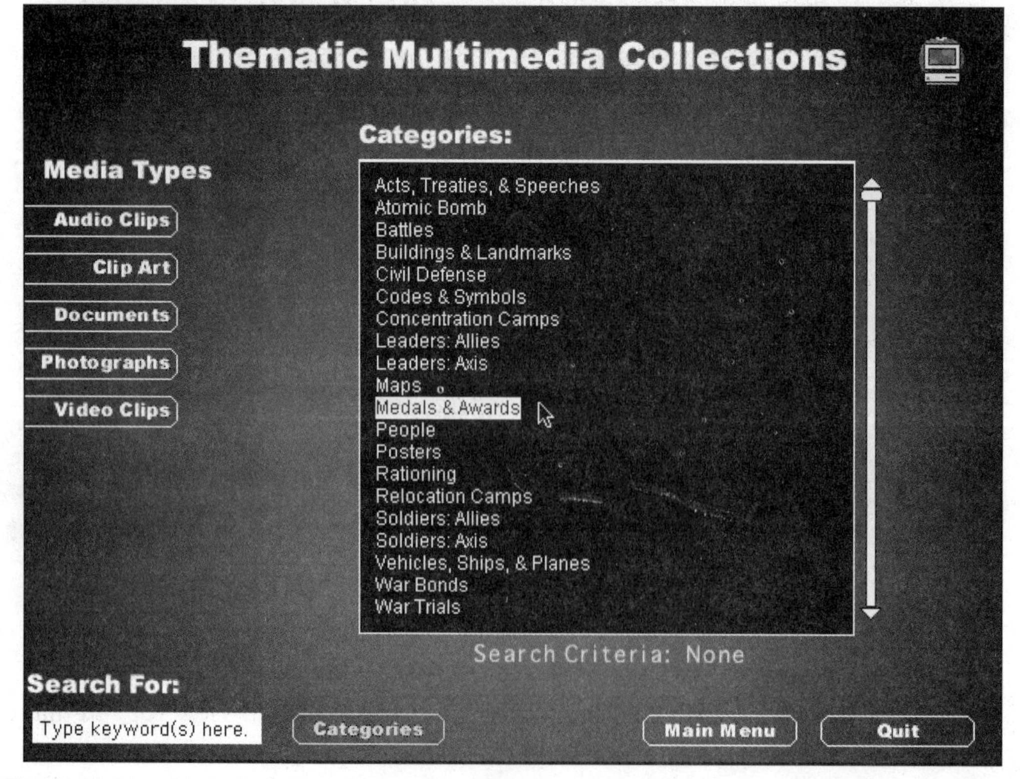

## Browsing by Category *(cont.)*

3. Click a title to listen to the audio clip or look at the picture, document, or video clip.

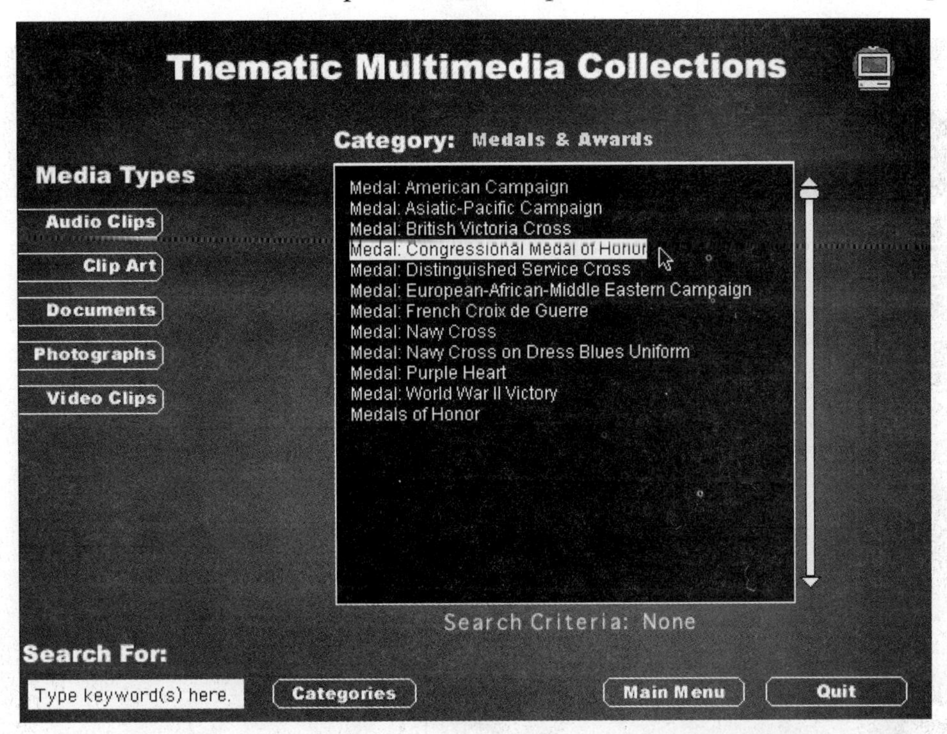


4. Click the **Back to List** button to return to the list. Click the **Right Arrow** to listen to the next audio clip or view the next picture, document, or video clip. Click the **Left Arrow** to go back to the previous item on the list.

5. Click the **Categories** button again and then click another category to view files in that category.

# Using the Viewer Program

## Copying and Pasting Photographs, Clip Art, and Text

The most efficient way to transfer photographs, clip art, and text from the viewer program into a document that you are working on is to copy and paste them. (*NOTE:* Audio and video files can be exported, but not copied and pasted; see pages 14 and 17.) Follow these easy steps to copy and paste.

1. Use the viewer to locate the photograph, clip art, or text that you want.
2. Click **Export** and choose **Copy to Clipboard**.

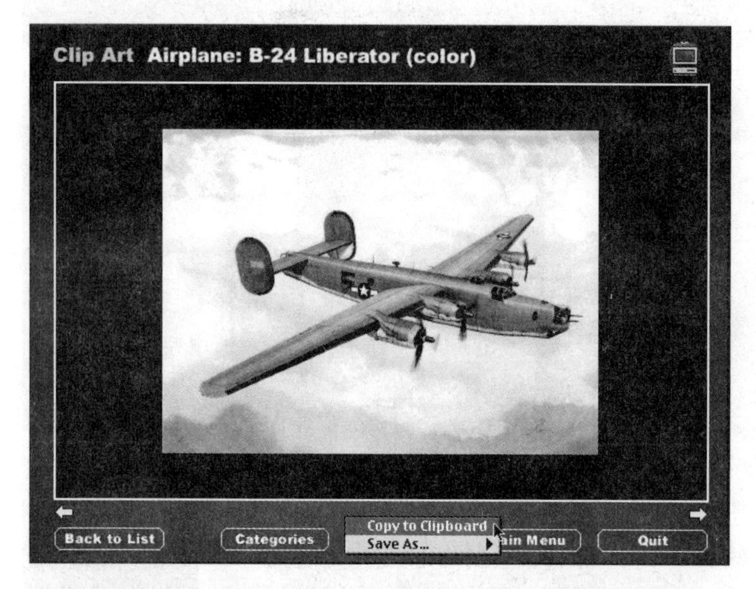


3. Click the **Desktop** button in the upper, right-hand corner to return to the computer's desktop.

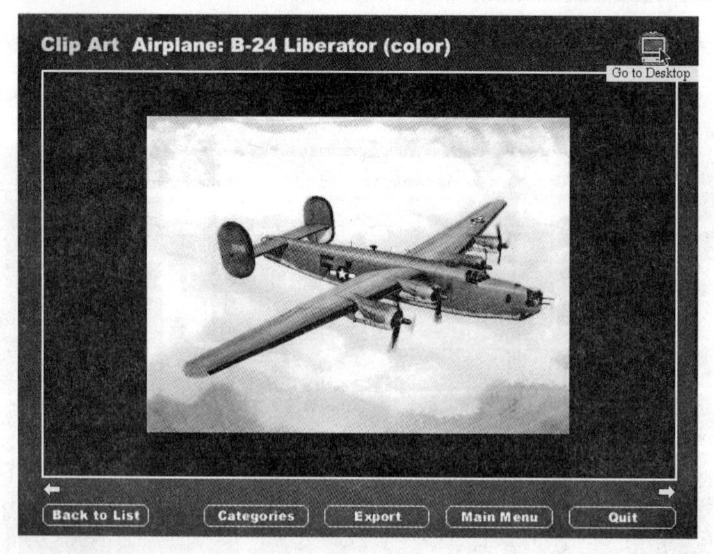


4. If you have not already done so, open the document in which you wish to add the media.
5. Choose **Paste** from the **Edit** menu in the application that you are using to create the document. To add more pictures, return to the viewer program and repeat the process. The viewer program continues to run in the background until you click **Quit**.

   *NOTE:* Some applications, such as *Microsoft PowerPoint*, require that you choose **Paste Special** from the **Edit** menu and then select the option Bitmap (BMP) or Picture (PICT).

## Copying and Pasting Photographs, Clip Art, and Text *(cont.)*

The viewer program provided on the multimedia CD also allows the user to easily save photograph or clip art files to several popular file formats, including BMP, EPS, GIF, JPEG, PICT, and TIFF. Follow these instructions to export files.

1. Click **Export** and choose **Save As...**

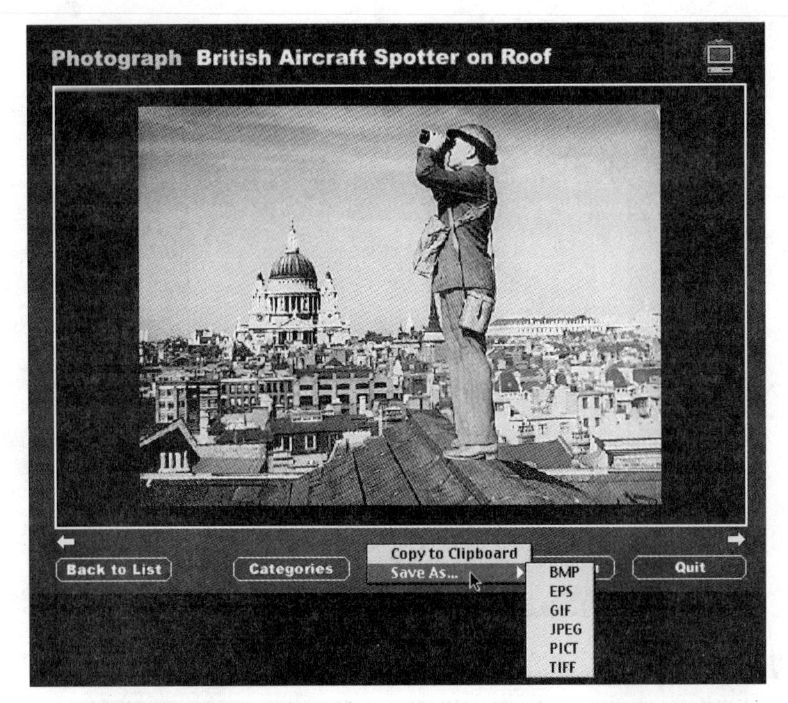


2. Choose the desired file format. (**GIF** export is not available on the Windows platform.)
3. Navigate to where you want to save the file (hard disk, floppy, etc.) and click **Save**.

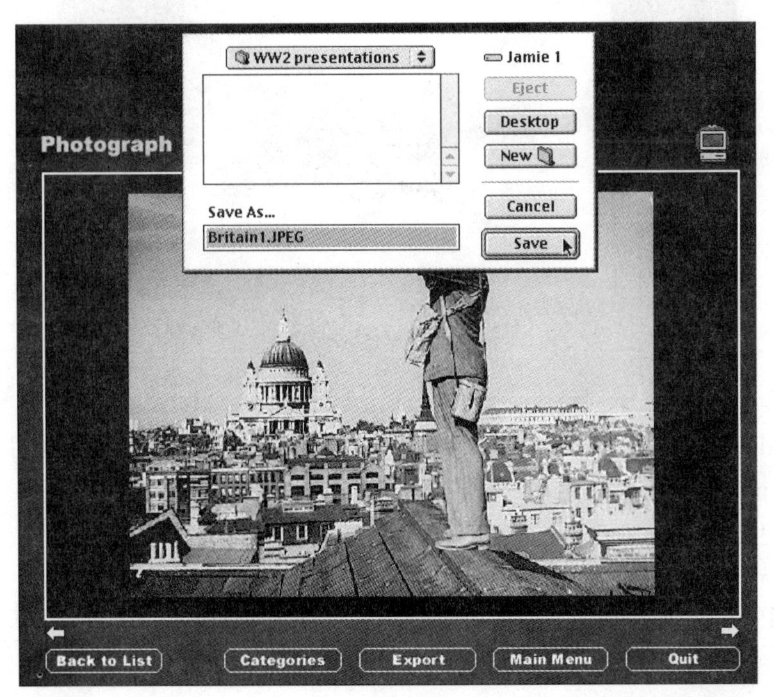

## Listening to and Exporting Audio Clips

**Media Types:** Click the **Audio Clips** button to view the list of audio clips (music, sound effects, etc.). Click any of the audio files listed to listen to them. These files have been provided in two formats: QuickTime and Wav. Consult your software documentation to find out which format works best for your application.

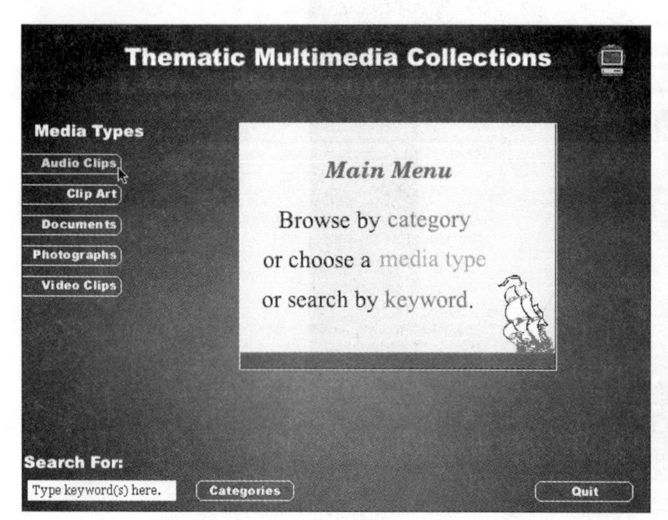


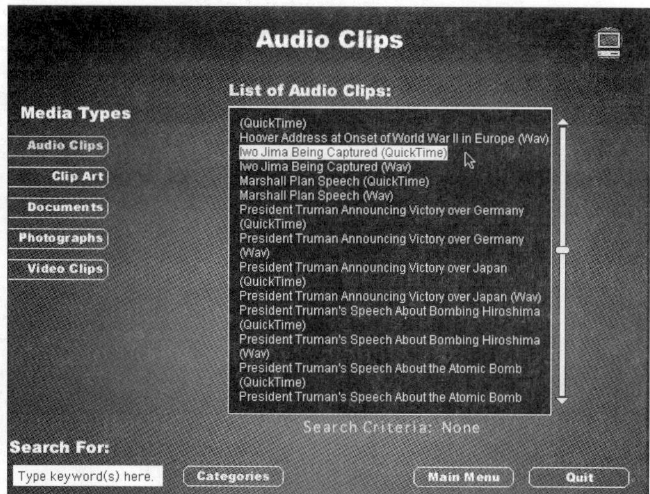


**Search For:** Type a keyword in the box here and press **Enter (Return)** to search only audio files.

**Export:** Click to export an audio clip for use in another program (see below). Navigate to where you want to save the file and click **Save**.

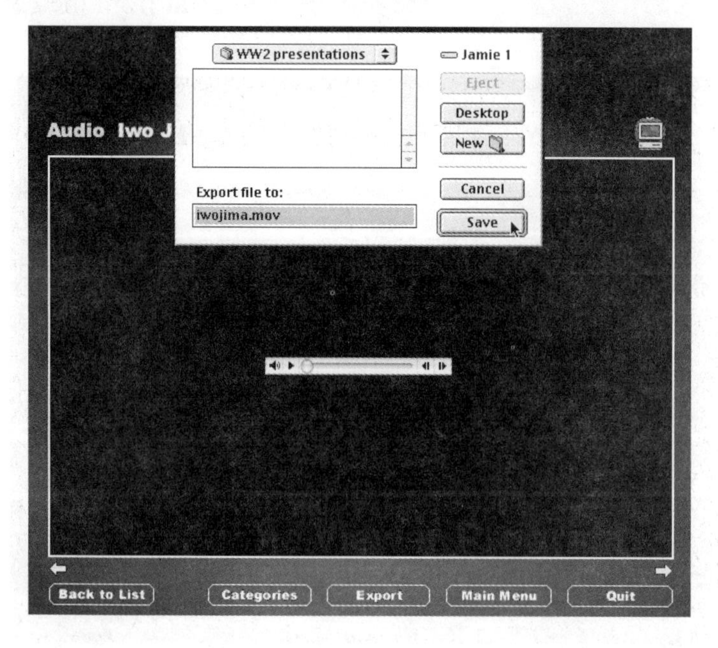


**Back to List:** Click to return to the list.

**Arrows:** Click the **Right Arrow** to go to the next audio clip and the **Left Arrow** to go to the previous one on the list.

**Main Menu:** Click to return to the main menu.

# Using the Viewer Program

## Viewing and Exporting Clip Art and Photographs

**Media Types:** Click the **Clip Art** or **Photographs** button to view the list of files. Click any of the clip art or photograph files listed to preview them.

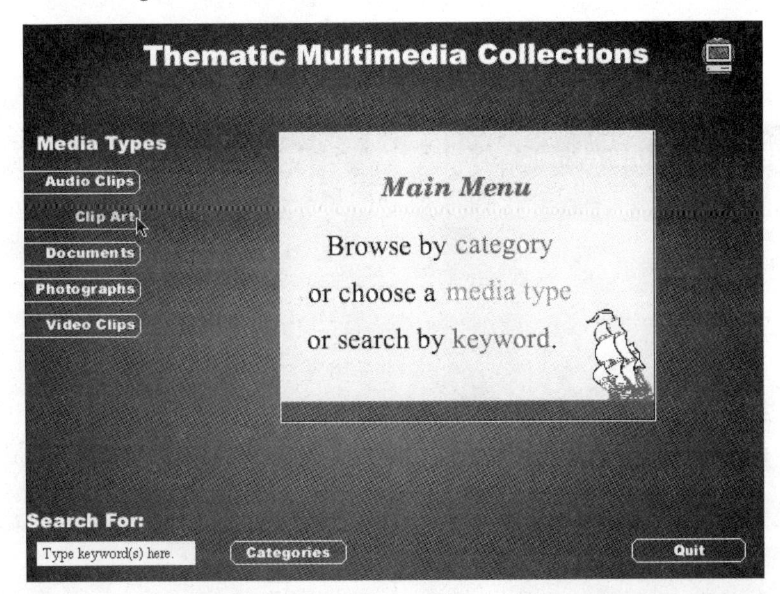


**Search For:** Type a keyword and press **Enter (Return)** to search only files in that media type.

**Export:** Click to export the image for use in another program. Choose **Copy to Clipboard** to copy and paste the image into another program, or choose **Save As...** and a file type to export the image for use in another program. (**GIF** export is not available on the Windows platform.) ***NOTE:*** Some applications, such as *Microsoft PowerPoint*, require that you choose **Paste Special** from the **Edit** menu and then select the option Bitmap (BMP) or Picture (PICT).

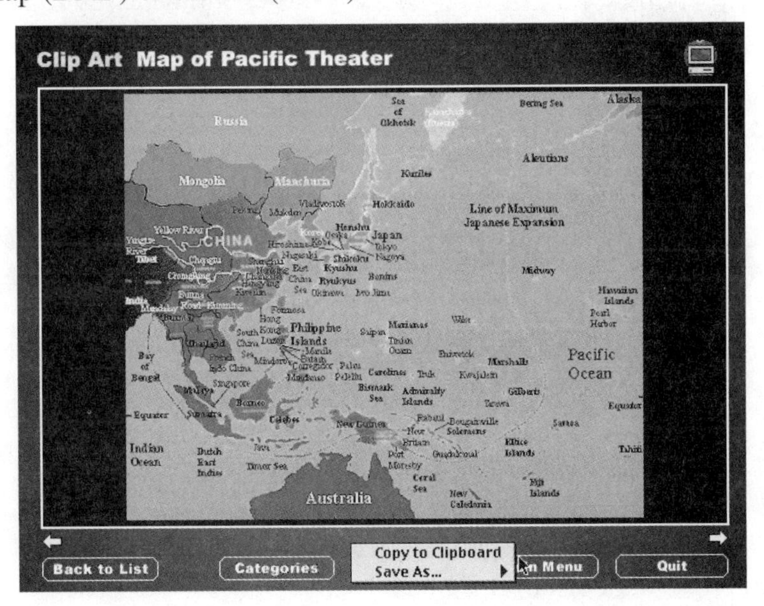


**Back to List:** Click to return to the list.

**Arrows:** Click the **Right Arrow** to see the next picture and the **Left Arrow** to go to the previous one on the list.

**Main Menu:** Click to return to the main menu.

## Viewing and Exporting Documents

**Media Types:** Click the **Documents** button to view the list of documents. Click any of the files listed to preview the document.

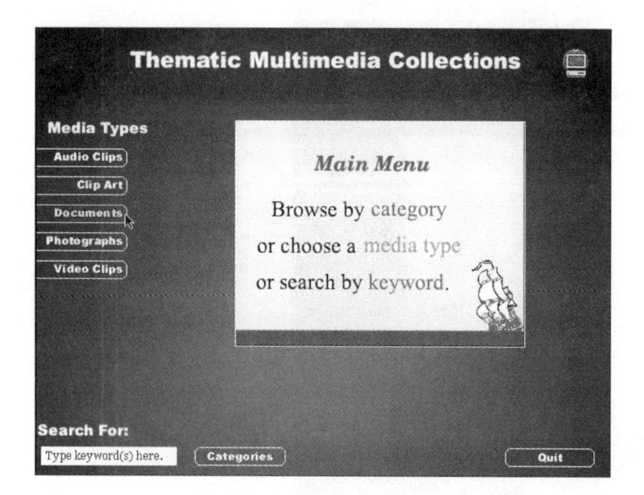


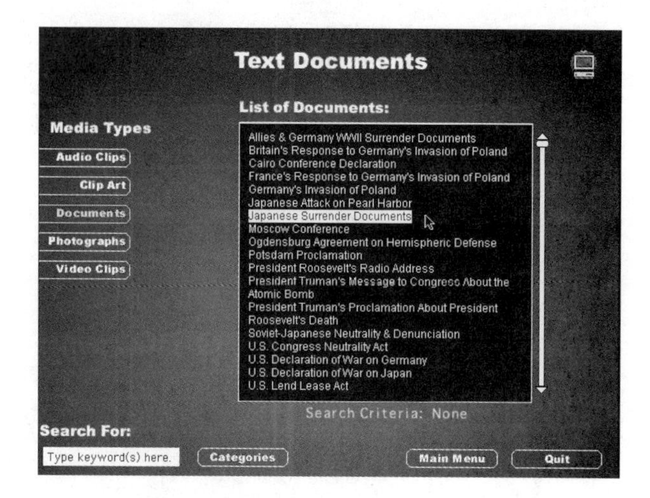


**Search For:** Type a keyword in the box and press **Enter (Return)** to search only the text documents.

**Export:** Click to export the text for use in another program. Choose **Export Text File** (below left) to copy the entire text of a document. Navigate to where you want to save the file and click **Save.**

Or, choose **Copy Selection to Clipboard** (below right) to copy and paste part of the text into another program. To select only part of the text, hold down the mouse button and highlight the desired text.

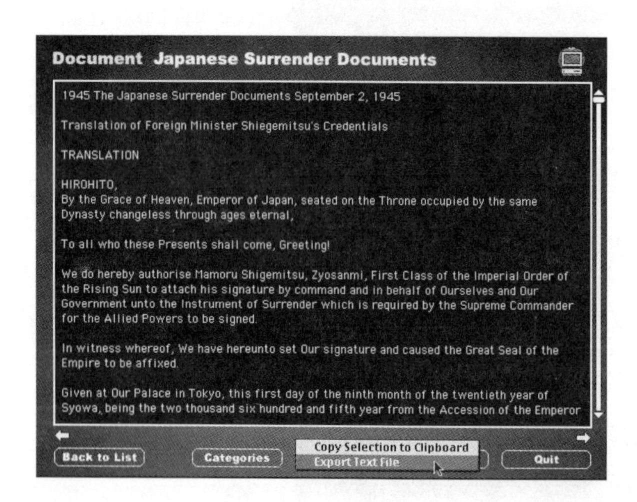


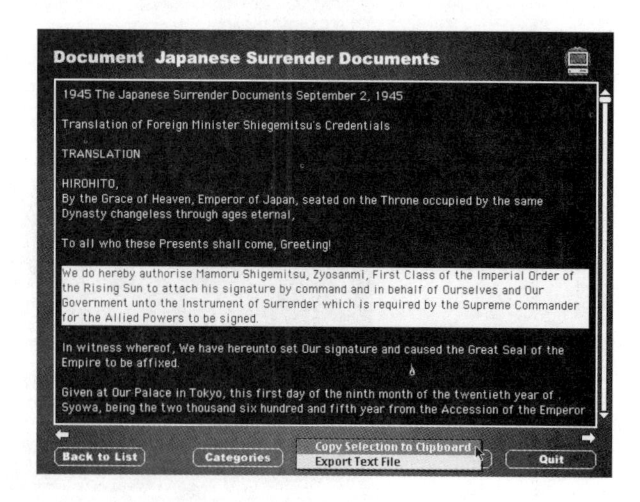


**Back to List:** Click to return to the list of documents.

**Arrows:** Click the **Right Arrow** to see the next document and the **Left Arrow** to go to the previous one on the list.

**Main Menu:** Click to return to the main menu.

## Viewing and Exporting Video Clips

**Media Types:** Click the **Video Clips** button to view the list of video clips. Click any of the video files listed to preview them. Video clips are provided in both QuickTime and AVI formats. Consult your software documentation to find out which format works best for your application. On the Windows platform, AVIs are the most compatible with *PowerPoint*.

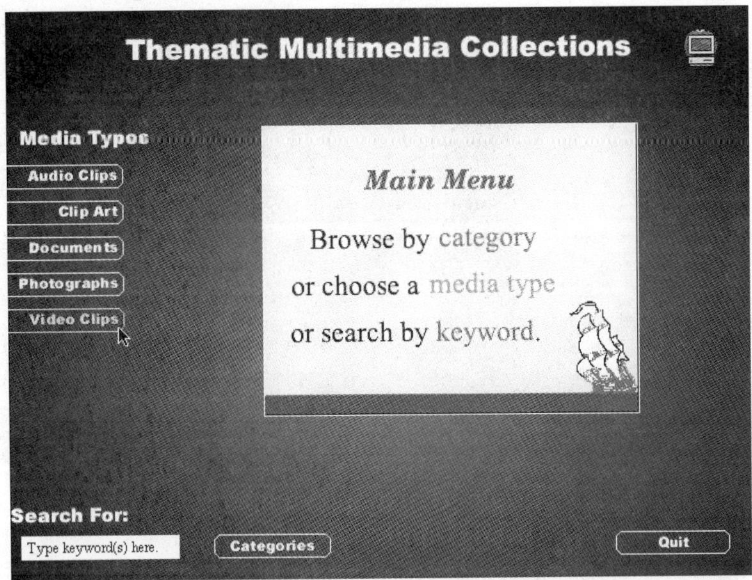


**Search For:** Type a keyword in the box and press **Enter (Return)** to search only video files.

**Export:** Click to export the video clip for use in another program. Navigate to where you want to save the file and click **Save**.

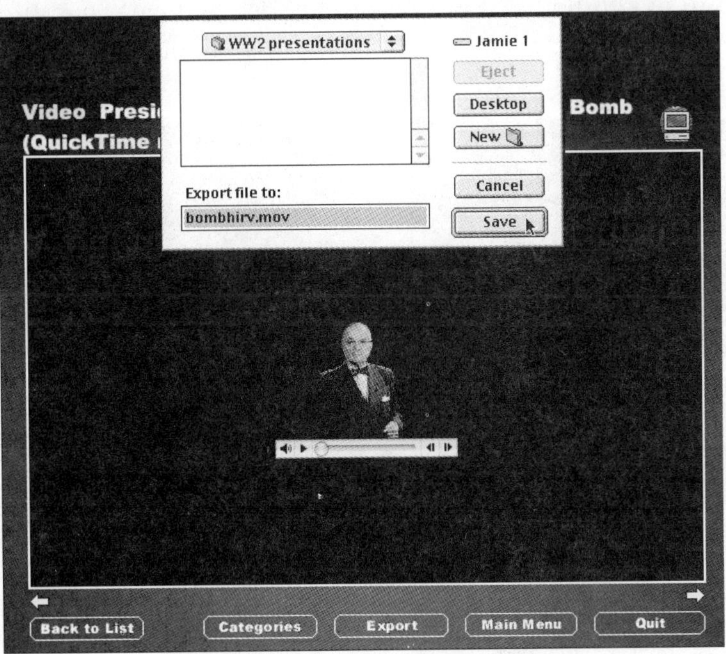


**Back to List:** Click to return to the list.

**Arrows:** Click the **Right Arrow** to see the next video and the **Left Arrow** to go to the previous one on the list.

**Main Menu:** Click to return to the main menu.

## Ideas for Using Multimedia Collections in the Classroom

### Teacher Uses

- Insert a series of photographs in a word-processing document and insert notes or captions. Print these on an overhead transparency and use them as visual aids.
- Use photos of people, places, and things as flashcards for students to study. For younger students, have them simply identify the photos. With older students, you can use the flashcards to have them identify the significance of the photographs.
- Import photos into a word-processing document to illustrate student work sheets. Have students explain the importance of the person, item, or event shown in the photos.

## Ideas for Using Multimedia Collections in the Classroom

### Teacher Uses *(cont.)*

- Create interactive practice activities using multimedia software such as *HyperStudio*.

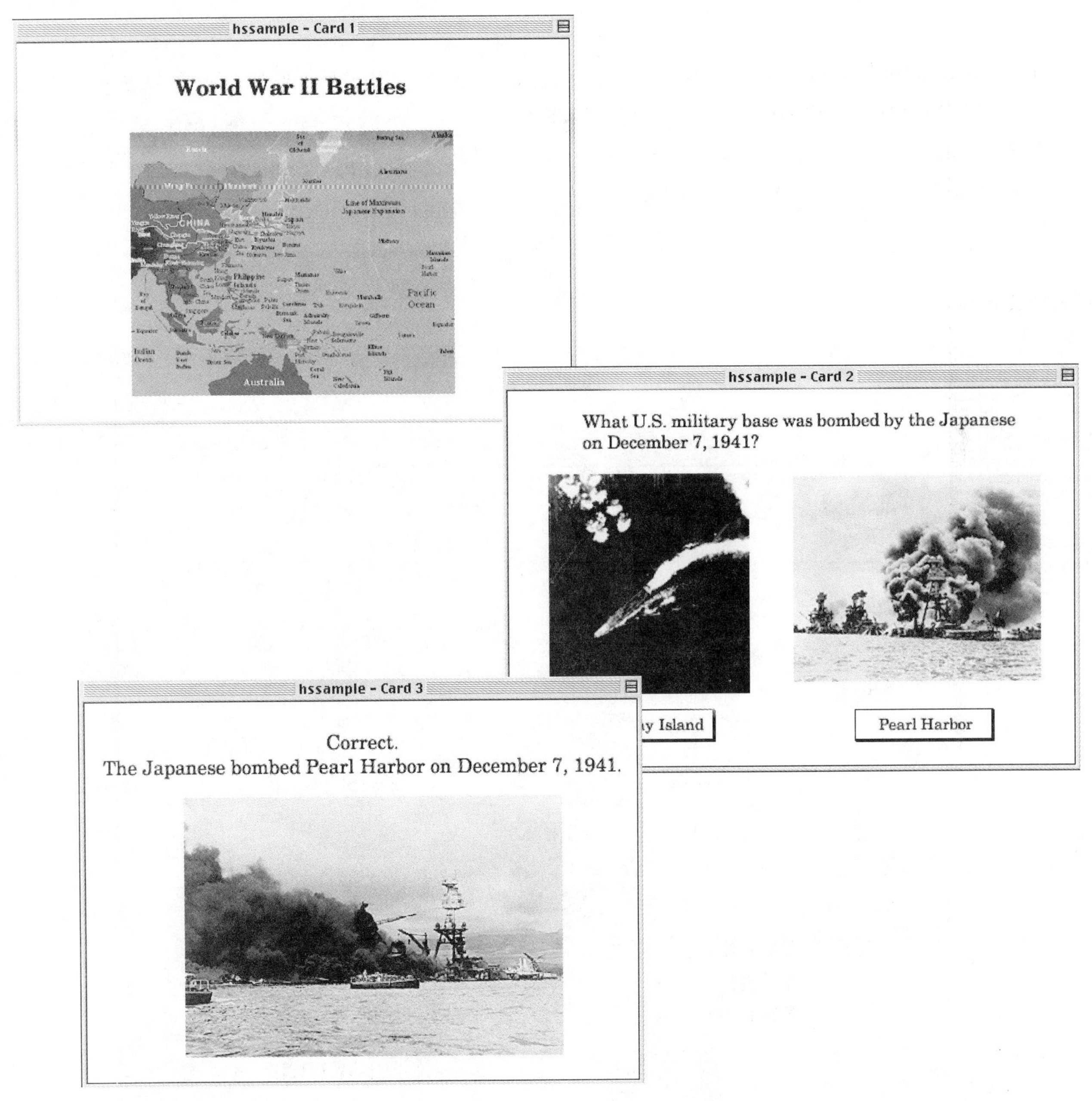


- Import a series of images into slide-show software such as *Microsoft PowerPoint*. Set the slide show to repeat itself on a computer at the front of the classroom or on a connected TV monitor. Use this simple slide show to grab students' attention as they walk into the classroom.
- Create a multimedia presentation using images and sound or video to illustrate your lesson.
- Make a Web page activity using the images and adding any hypertext links to sites you want your students to visit. Save the Web page to a folder on your hard drive so students can view it quickly. Include sounds or video clips to add more interest.

## Teacher Uses *(cont.)*

- Open a video file in your Web browser for students to play at a learning center in your classroom. Provide students with several questions to answer about the images they see. You could also create a Web page with the questions and video file on one screen.

  ***NOTE:*** The HTML code for embedding a *QuickTime* movie file in a Web page is

  <embed src="file:///drive/folder/file" width="320" height="255" autoplay="true">

  where width is the width in pixels of the actual movie and height is the movie height plus about 15 pixels for the *QuickTime* bar at the bottom of the movie. The file location would be wherever you have saved it on your computer's hard drive.

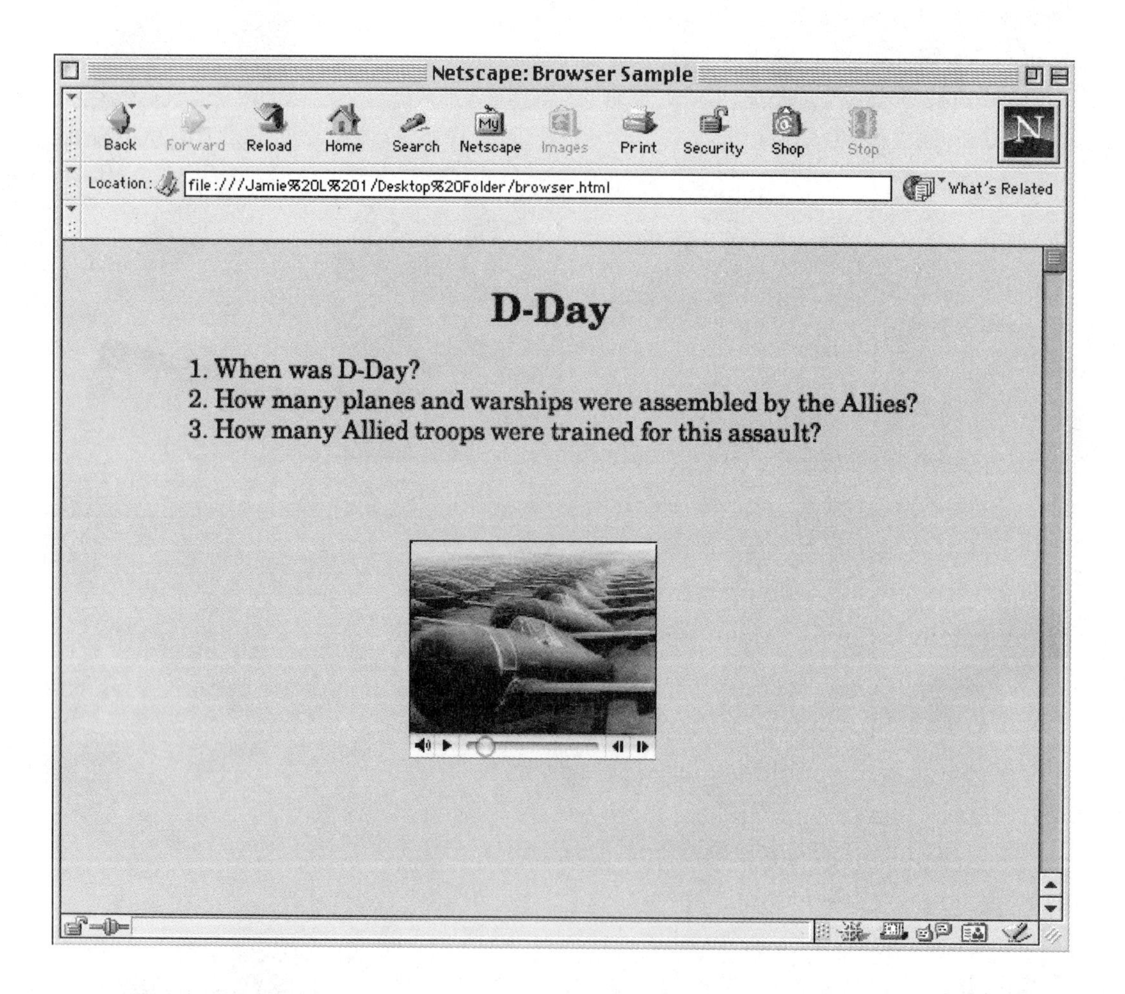


- Print a photo using word-processing or sign-making software and use it as a bulletin board weekly challenge. Have a "suggestion box" under the photo and let students write their names and guesses on paper and insert them in the box. Use that same image as part of a lesson once you have pulled all the entries out of the box. Award a monthly prize to the students with the most correct guesses. Create a certificate using all four of that month's challenge photos.

# Ideas for Using Multimedia Collections in the Classroom

## Student Uses

- Have students create diagrams by importing photos or clip art into a paint or draw program. Use the line and text tools to label parts or call attention to details.
- Students can import the images and other files into multimedia presentations rather than writing typical reports about the topic.
- Have students make posters about the people, places, and events of a particular time period. They can import a photo into word-processing or sign-making software such as *Microsoft® Works*, *AppleWorks* (formerly known as *ClarisWorks*), or *Print Shop*. Once they have researched the subject in the photo, they can create their posters and include important pieces of information.

- Students can make period newspapers. Have them use newsletter-making software or word-processing software to create newspapers for the time period they are studying. They can then import the photos or clip-art images to illustrate their articles.
- Let teams of students create challenges for each other. Have them use simple photo-editing software to add special effects to portraits of famous people in order to stump the opposing teams as they try to guess who the people are.

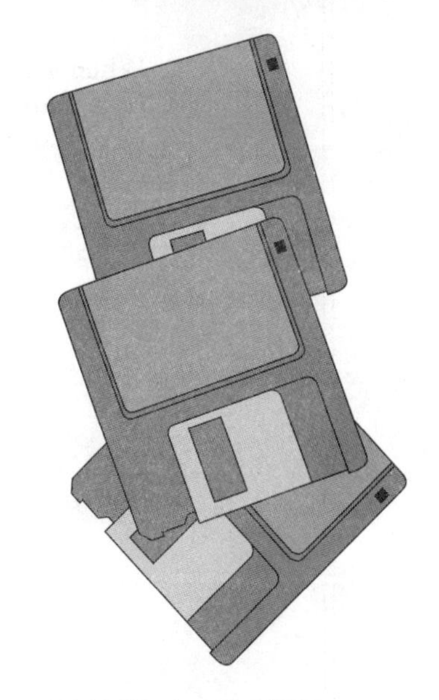

- Students can create multimedia presentations based on various songs included in the sound files. They can find the lyrics to the songs and use them as the headings on slides, adding photos that help illustrate the songs.
- Have student teams create multimedia presentations for a special technology parent night. Have them use the image, video, and sound files to create *HyperStudio* (or other multimedia program) presentations about what they have learned during their study of a particular topic. If you have a computer lab, have the students save their projects to various computers around the room. If you don't have a lab, try to get a projector or television connector so you can show the program to the entire classroom. Invite parents to come and have the students show off their presentations. You might want to invite the principal and board of education members to this event as well.

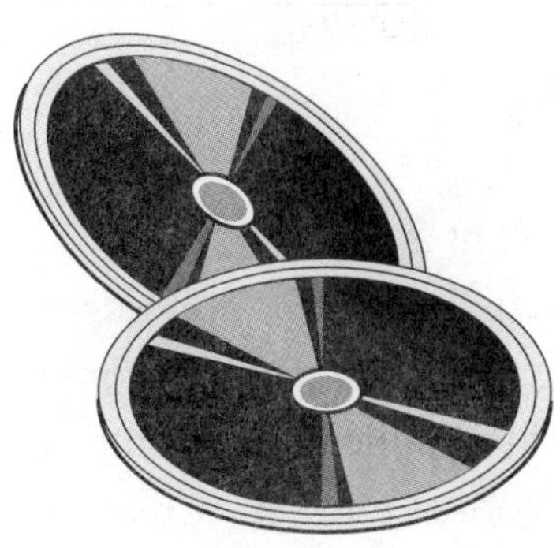

## Student Uses *(cont.)*

- Students can write stories based on particular images. Have them import the images at the top of a word-processing document and then write about what is happening.
- Assign topics to the students and have them write research papers and import several images to help illustrate the topic. This is a great way to practice their word-processing skills.

- Have groups of students create multimedia presentations to "teach the class" about a concept you are studying. Each group in the class can have a different concept. They can use the image, sound, and video files in their multimedia presentations. You can keep these presentations on your classroom computer for students to use as review before tests.
- Have students create slide shows using *PowerPoint*, *HyperStudio*, or another multimedia program and add their own narration rather than entering text into each slide. This may take some planning in order to find a quiet place in your room or a computer lab area for them to do the recording.

- Students could also present the "Morning News" in your classroom, using news clips from the time period you are studying. They could use the images and video files to represent the "filmed event" they are reporting. Videotape the students reporting the news with the computer monitor sitting behind them and facing toward the audience (and video camera).
- At the end of the year, have students create a multimedia presentation on "What We Learned This Year" to present to the next year's class. They could incorporate previous multimedia presentations or start from scratch and create a new project.

# Thumbnail Photo Images and Clip Art

nagumo1.jpg

Admiral Chuichi Nagumo

moto3.jpg

Admiral Isoroku Yamamoto

moto2.jpg

Admiral Isoroku Yamamoto Plotting Course on Chart

moto1.jpg

Admiral Isoroku Yamamoto Poster

eichmann.jpg

Adolf Eichmann

hitler5.jpg

Adolf Hitler & Benito Mussolini

hitler1.jpg

Adolf Hitler Poster

hitler4.jpg

Adolf Hitler Viewing Damage

goeb1.jpg

Adolf Hitler with Goering, Goebbels, & Hess

airraid2.jpg

Air Raid Instructions

airraid1.jpg

Air Raid Instructions for Schools

airraid3.jpg

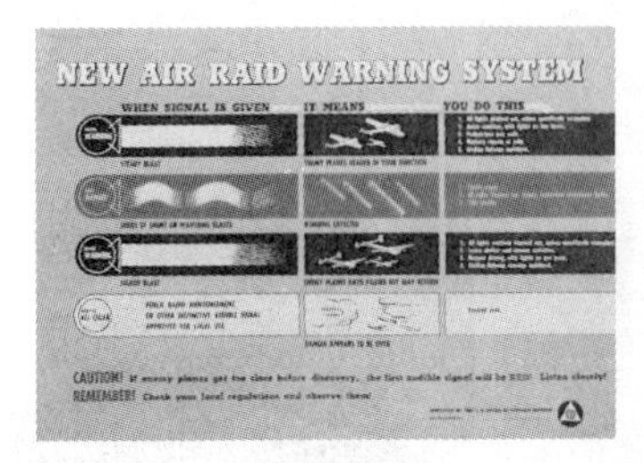


Air Raid Warning System

## Thumbnail Photo Images and Clip Art

plane.jpg

Airplane and Pilot

b17-a.jpg

Airplane: B-17 Flying Fortress

b17.jpg

Airplane: B-17 Flying Fortress at Airstrip

b17-b.jpg

Airplane: B-17 Flying Fortress (color)

b-17-1.jpg

Airplane: B-17 Flying Fortress Preparing for Takeoff

belle7.jpg

Airplane: B-17 Memphis Belle

belle3.jpg

Airplane: B-17 Memphis Belle Cockpit

belle5.jpg

Airplane: B-17 Memphis Belle Crew

belle8.jpg

Airplane: B-17 Memphis Belle Flying

belle1.jpg

Airplane: B-17 Memphis Belle Guns at Windows

belle2.jpg

Airplane: B-17 Memphis Belle in Museum

belle6.jpg

Airplane: B-17 Memphis Belle Interior

# Thumbnail Photo Images and Clip Art

belle4.jpg

Airplane: B-17 Memphis Belle Interior Gun Mounts

b24.jpg

Airplane: B-24 Liberator

b24-3.jpg

Airplane: B-24 Liberator at Airfield

b24-b.jpg

Airplane: B-24 Liberator (color)

b24-1.jpg

Airplane: B-24 Liberator Flying

b24-2.jpg

Airplane: B-24 Liberator on Runway

bockscar.jpg

Airplane: B-29 Bockscar

b29-3.jpg

Airplane: B-29 Superfortress

b-29-4.jpg

Airplane: B-29 Superfortress at Airport

b29-1.jpg

Airplane: B-29 Superfortress by Hangar

b29-2.jpg

Airplane: B-29 Superfortress (interior)

enola1.jpg

Airplane: Enola Gay

# Thumbnail Photo Images and Clip Art

enola2.jpg

Airplane: Enola Gay at Airfield

corsair1.jpg

Airplane: F4U-1D Corsair

corsair2.jpg

Airplane: F4U-1D Corsair Firing

corsair.jpg

Airplane: F4U-1D Corsair Flying

grum3.jpg

Airplane: Grumman F3F-1 Fighter

grum2.jpg

Airplane: Grumman F3F-2 Fighter

grum1.jpg

Airplane: Grumman F3F-3 Fighter

avenger1.jpg

Airplane: Grumman TBF-1 Avenger

spitfire.jpg

Airplane: Spitfire

einstein.jpg

Albert Einstein

scrap6.jpg

America Needs Your Scrap Rubber Poster

amflag2.jpg

American Flag Poster

## Thumbnail Photo Images and Clip Art

cemetery.jpg

American Soldiers Cemetery in Normandy, France

cemeter2.jpg

American Soldiers Cemetery & Soldiers Paying Tribute

fatman1.jpg

Atomic Bomb "Fatman" (Nagasaki)

lit-boy1.jpg

Atomic Bomb "Little Boy" (Hiroshima)

trinity.jpg

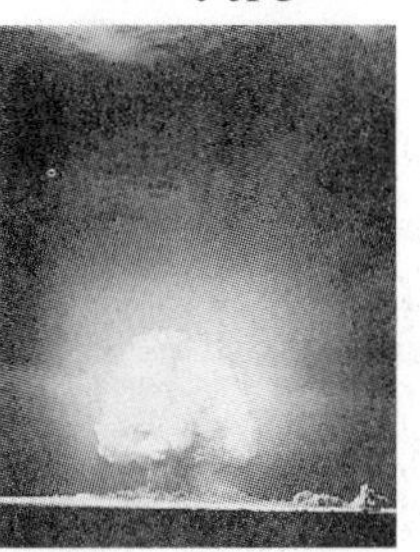

Atomic Bomb Mushroom Cloud at Trinity Test Site

ausch4.jpg

Auschwitz: Children Behind Barbed Wire

concen4.jpg

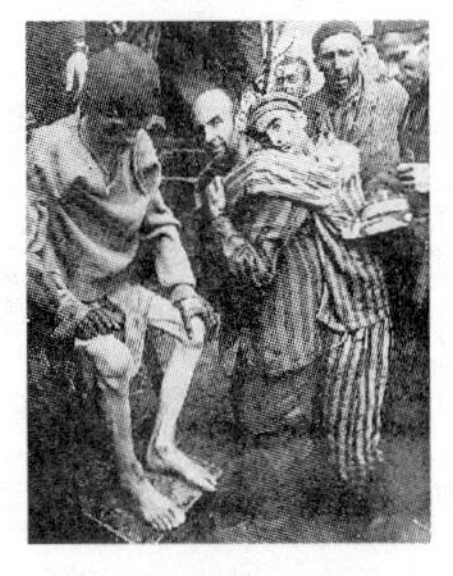

Auschwitz: Men

ausch1.jpg

Auschwitz: Men Behind Fences

concen3.jpg

Auschwitz: Men in Barracks

ausch3.jpg

Auschwitz: Women in Barracks

midway2.jpg

Battle of Midway: Aerial View

midway1.jpg

Battle of Midway: Bombers Flying

## Thumbnail Photo Images and Clip Art

midway3.jpg

Battle of Midway: Ground View

midway4.jpg

Battle of Midway: Ships Being Bombed

midway5.jpg

Battle of Midway: Smoke From Ship

britain4.jpg

British Air Raid Shelter 1

britain3.jpg

British Air Raid Shelter 2

britain1.jpg

British Aircraft Spotter on Roof

degaul1.jpg

Charles de Gaulle on Balcony

truman6.jpg

Charles de Gaulle with Harry Truman

chiang1.jpg

Chiang Kai-Shek, Roosevelt, & Churchill

ration3.jpg

Children Using Ration Books to Purchase Groceries

mao2.jpg

Chinese Listening to Mao Tse-tung Speech

big3b.jpg

Churchill, Roosevelt, & Stalin

# Thumbnail Photo Images and Clip Art

coloss.jpg

Colosseum in Rome

bergen4.jpg

Concentration Camp Crematorium

bergen3.jpg

Concentration Camp Interior

bergen1.jpg

Concentration Camp Prisoners Working Outside

dday1.jpg

D-Day Invasion at Normandy, France 1

dday2.jpg

D-Day Invasion at Normandy, France 2

dday3.jpg

D-Day Invasion of Normandy Poster 1

dday4.jpg

D-Day Invasion of Normandy Poster 2

dwight2.jpg

Dwight D. Eisenhower

dwight3.jpg

Dwight D. Eisenhower Boarding Airplane

dwight1.jpg

Dwight & Mamie Eisenhower Leaving Plane

eleanor1.jpg

Eleanor Roosevelt

## Thumbnail Photo Images and Clip Art

eleanor2.jpg

Eleanor Roosevelt with Mrs. Churchill

eleanor3.jpg

Eleanor Roosevelt & Wounded Soldier

hirohito.jpg

Emperor Hirohito

rommel1.jpg

Erwin Rommel

semaphor.jpg

Flag Code Practice (Semaphore)

fdr1.jpg

Franklin Delano Roosevelt

fdr2.jpg

Franklin Delano Roosevelt Campaign Poster

macarth1.jpg

General Douglas MacArthur

macarth2.jpg

General Douglas MacArthur Wading Ashore at Leyte

arnold1.jpg

General Henry "Hap" Arnold

ger-dest.jpg

German Battleship Destroyer

enigma.jpg

German Enigma Code Machine

 

# Thumbnail Photo Images and Clip Art

britain2.jpg

German Luftwaffe Bombed London

warsaw3.jpg

German Soldiers Arresting People in Warsaw Ghetto

warsaw2.jpg

German Soldiers Guarding Warsaw Ghetto Families

warsaw4.jpg

German Soldiers Marching

warsaw5.jpg

German Soldiers Patrolling Warsaw Ghetto

germsub1.jpg

German Submarine

uboat.jpg

German U-Boat Under Attack by B-24

gun2.jpg

Gun: 240mm Howitzer & Artillery Crew

garand3.jpg

Gun: M1 Garand Rifle

gun.jpg

Gun: Turret Gun Bunker

himmler1.jpg

Heinrich Himmler

goering1.jpg

Hermann Goering

# Thumbnail Photo Images and Clip Art

hiro4.jpg

Hiroshima: Atomic Bomb Mushroom Cloud

hiro5.jpg

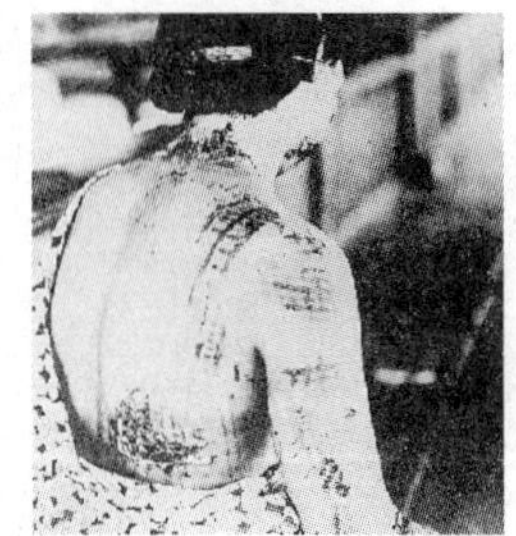

Hiroshima: Atomic Bomb Radiation Damage (Back)

hiro1.jpg

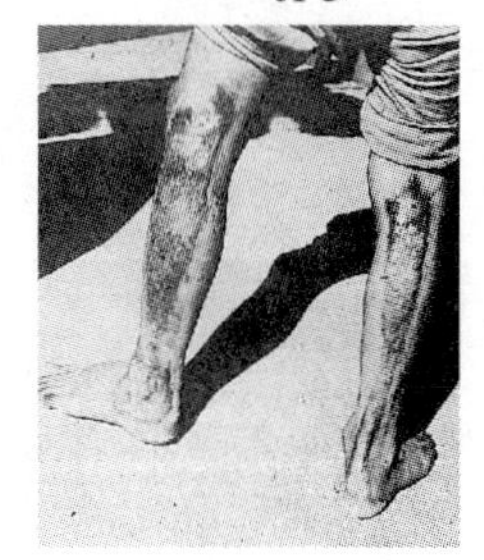

Hiroshima: Atomic Bomb Radiation Damage (Legs)

hiro3.jpg

Hiroshima: Man with Radiation Sickness

h-youth1.jpg

Hitler Youth

j-army.jpg

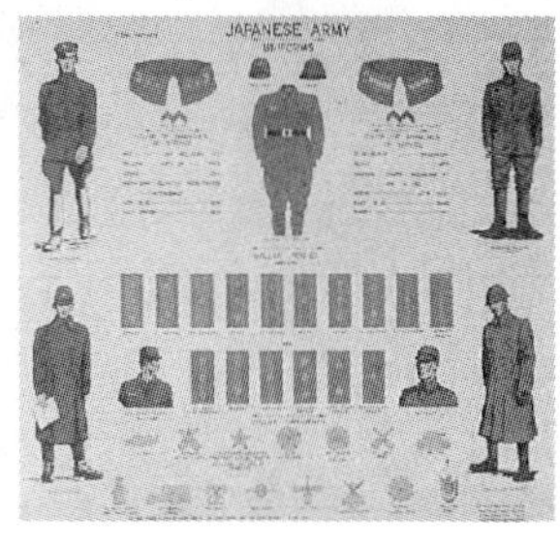


Japanese Army Uniforms

shim1.jpg

Japanese Battleship

camp1.jpg

Japanese Relocation Camp in U.S.

scouts2.jpg

Japanese Relocation Camp in U.S.— Boy Scouts

camp3.jpg

Japanese Relocation Camp in U.S.— Children 1

camp4.jpg

Japanese Relocation Camp in U.S.— Children 2

camp2.jpg

Japanese Relocation Camp in U.S.— Man & Child

 

# Thumbnail Photo Images and Clip Art

j-sub1.jpg

Japanese Submarine

miss1.jpg

Japanese Surrender Documents Being Signed on the U.S.S. Missouri

golden.jpg

Japanese Temple of the Golden Pavilion

jeep5.jpg

Jeep Bouncing Along Rough Terrain

jeep3.jpg

Jeep Campaign in Schools Poster

jeep4.jpg

Jeep Transporting Wounded Soldiers

jfk.jpg

John F. Kennedy

jfkmed.jpg

John F. Kennedy Receiving Medal

stalin1.jpg

Joseph Stalin

kremlin.jpg

Kremlin

kristal1.jpg

Kristalnacht: Night of Broken Glass

britain5.jpg

London After German Bombing

# Thumbnail Photo Images and Clip Art

bigben1.jpg

London's Big Ben & Barbed Wire

mao1.jpg

Mao Tse-tung Speaking to Crowd

map.jpg

Map of Europe 1944

pacific.jpg

Map of Pacific

europe.jpg

Map of the Eastern Front Battle Area

pacific1.jpg

Map of the Pacific & Far East

acsm.jpg

Medal: American Campaign

apcm.jpg

Medal: Asiatic-Pacific Campaign

vcbig.jpg

Medal: British Victoria Cross

mcmh.jpg

Medal: Congressional Medal of Honor

dscm.jpg

Medal: Distinguished Service Cross

eamesm.jpg

Medal: European-African-Middle Eastern Campaign

 

# Thumbnail Photo Images and Clip Art

croix.jpg

Medal: French Croix de Guerre

nc2.jpg

Medal: Navy Cross

nc3.jpg

Medal: Navy Cross on Dress Blues Uniform

prplhrt.jpg

Medal: Purple Heart

ww2vic.jpg

Medal: World War II Victory

moh.jpg

Medals of Honor

forms.jpg

Men in Uniform Poster

nagasaki.jpg

Nagasaki Atomic Explosion

naga1.jpg

Nagasaki Bomb Damage

navatalk.jpg

Navajo Code Talkers

neville.jpg

Neville Chamberlain

pacific2.jpg

NewsMap War Fronts: Pacific 1

## Thumbnail Photo Images and Clip Art

pacific3.jpg

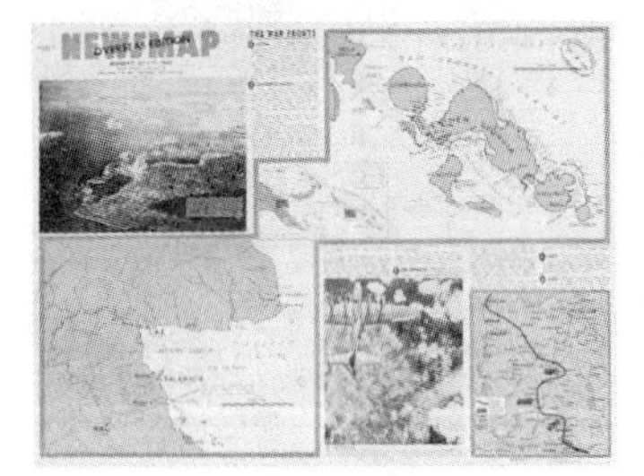


NewsMap War Fronts: Pacific 2

freedom2.jpg

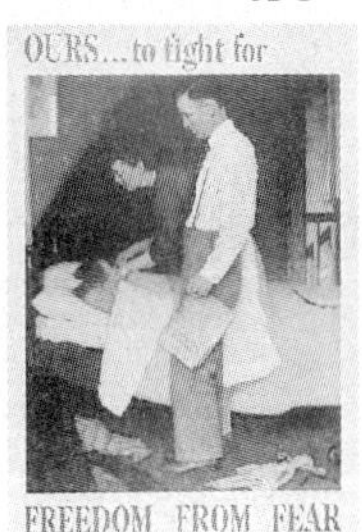


Norman Rockwell: Freedom from Fear Poster

freedom3.jpg

Norman Rockwell: Freedom from Want Poster

freedom4.jpg

Norman Rockwell: Freedom of Speech Poster

freedom5.jpg

Norman Rockwell: Freedom of Worship Poster

trials1.jpg

Nuremburg Trials

trials4.jpg

Nuremburg Trials Holding Cell & Guard

trials2.jpg

Nuremburg Trials Holding Cells

trials3.jpg

Nuremburg Trials: Nazi War Criminals

arizona2.jpg

Pearl Harbor: Arizona After Bombing

arizona1.jpg

Pearl Harbor: Arizona Sinking

phattack.jpg

Pearl Harbor Attack (color)

 

# Thumbnail Photo Images and Clip Art

pearl6.jpg

Pearl Harbor: Explosion on Ships

pearl3.jpg

Pearl Harbor: Ships Being Bombed

pearl5.jpg

Pearl Harbor: Ships' Billowing Smoke

pearl4.jpg

Pearl Harbor: Smoke From Bombed Ships

pearl2.jpg

Pearl Harbor: Smoke From Bombs

pearl1.jpg

Pearl Harbor: Soldiers Watching Bombing at Airstrip

zyklon3.jpg

Poison Gas Canisters

zyklon1.jpg

Poison Gas Canisters & Gas Mask

zyklon2.jpg

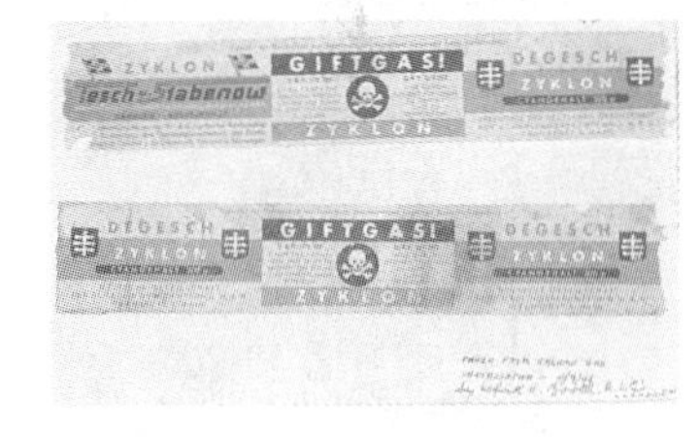


Poison Gas Labels

scrap3.jpg

Poster: Scraps Wanted

truman1.jpg

President Truman Inspecting Troops

truman3.jpg

President Truman With Officers

## Thumbnail Photo Images and Clip Art

truman2.jpg

President Truman With Winston Churchill 1

truman4.jpg

President Truman With Winston Churchill 2

ptboat.jpg

PT Boat

ration10.jpg

Ration Book

ration1.jpg

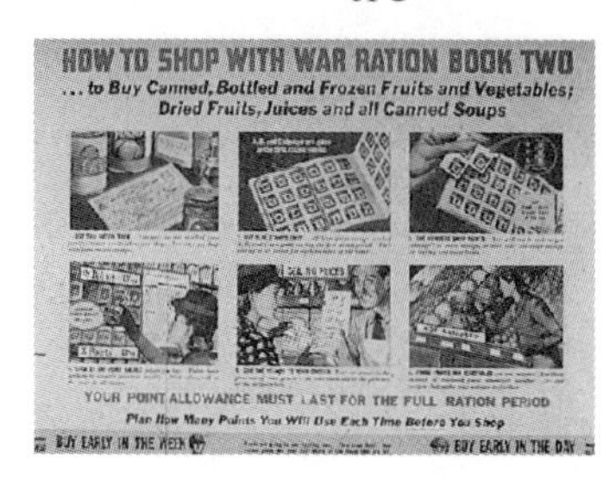


Ration Book Poster

scrap5.jpg

Rationing at Home Poster

ration4.jpg

Rationing: Boy Buying Juice

hitler3.jpg

Rationing: Car Sharing Poster

ration2.jpg

Rationing Explained to Students

scrap1.jpg

Rationing: Farm Scraps Build Destroyers Poster

ration7.jpg

Rationing: Food Canning Poster

ration6.jpg

Rationing Helps Soldiers Poster

## Thumbnail Photo Images and Clip Art

ration5.jpg

Rationing Point Values of Meat

ration8.jpg

Rationing Poster

scrap4.jpg

Rationing: Save Waste Fats Poster

ration11.jpg

Rationing Saves Lives Poster

scrap2.jpg

Rationing: Stop Fuel Waste Poster

ration9.jpg

Rationing: Sugar Allowance Coupons

ration12.jpg

Rationing: Victory Garden Poster

cross5.jpg

Red Cross Motor Corps Poster

cross2.jpg

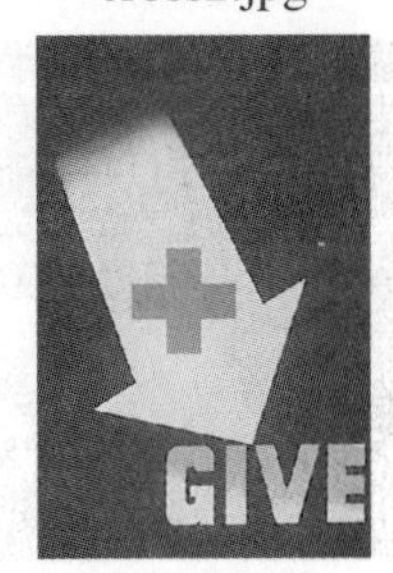


Red Cross Poster

cross6.jpg

Red Cross & Soldier Poster

cross4.jpg

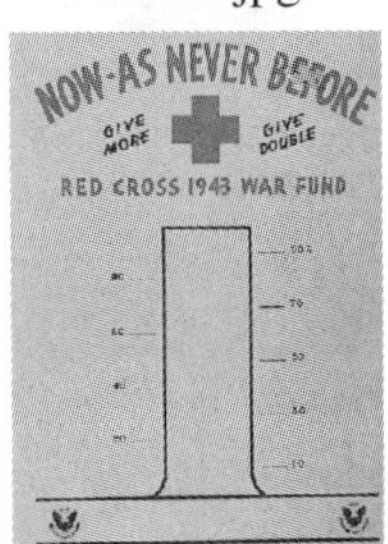


Red Cross War Fund Poster

cross3.jpg

Red Cross Workers Poster

# Thumbnail Photo Images and Clip Art

cross1.jpg

Red Cross Workers Tending Wounded Soldiers

reich1.jpg

Reichstag

reich2.jpg

Reichstag Interior

oppen1.jpg

Robert Oppenheimer (Manhattan Project)

rosie4.jpg

Rosie the Riveter Poster

iwojima2.jpg

Ships Landing at Iwo Jima

garand1.jpg

Soldier Next to Tank

austral.jpg

Soldier Poster: Australian

canadian.jpg

Soldier Poster: Canadian

chinese.jpg

Soldier Poster: Chinese

dutch.jpg

Soldier Poster: Dutch

english.jpg

Soldier Poster: English

# Thumbnail Photo Images and Clip Art

ethiopia.jpg

Soldier Poster: Ethiopian

russian.jpg

Soldier Poster: Russian

garand2.jpg

Soldier With Rifle

mural.jpg

Soldiers

bulge1.jpg

Soldiers at the Battle of the Bulge

letter1.jpg

Soldiers Need Letters Poster

letter2.jpg

Soldiers Reading Letters From Home

big3.jpg

Stalin, Roosevelt, & Churchill

david.jpg

Star of David

swastika.jpg

Swastika

tank5.jpg

Tank

tank4.jpg

Tank: Allied

# Thumbnail Photo Images and Clip Art

paris.jpg

Tank Crew Enters Paris
After Liberation

tank.jpg

Tank in Street

85-2.jpg

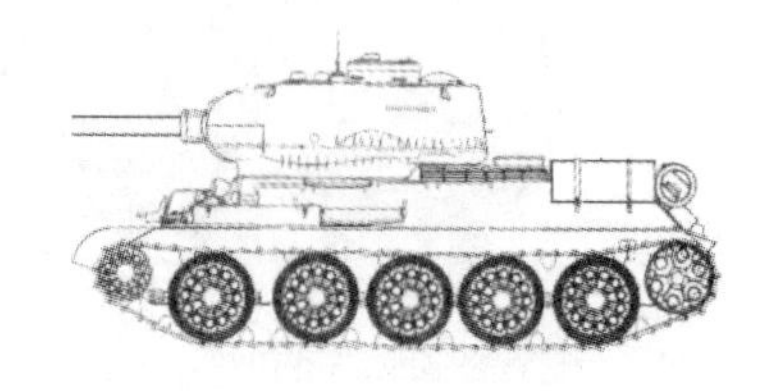

Tank: Russian T-34

tank3.jpg

Tank & U.S. Soldiers

tank2.jpg

Tank with Soldier

nations1.jpg

United Nations Fight For
Freedom Poster 1

nations2.jpg

United Nations Fight For
Freedom Poster 2

nations3.jpg

United Nations Fight For
Freedom Poster 3

guard3.jpg

U.S. Army Female Desk
Sergeant

guard2.jpg

U.S. Army Female
Soldier

guard1.jpg

U.S. Army Male Soldier

ballard1.jpg

U.S. Battleship Ballard

 

# Thumbnail Photo Images and Clip Art

peterson.jpg

U.S. Battleship Peterson

york1.jpg

U.S. Battleship Yorktown

capitol1.jpg

U.S. Capitol Building

machgun.jpg

U.S. Gunner on PT Boat

soldier3.jpg

U.S. Jungle Fighters

iwojima3.jpg

U.S. Marine Standing Near Flag on Iwo Jima

gasmask1.jpg

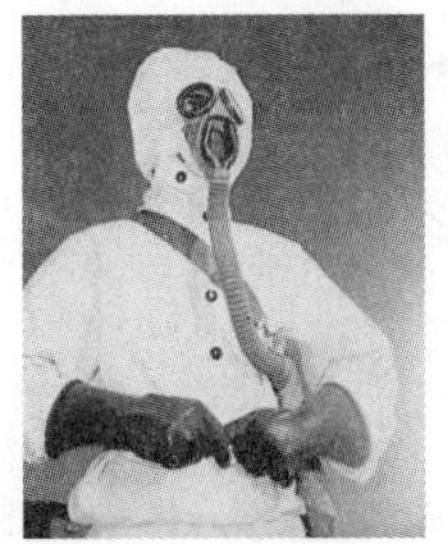

U.S. Marine Wearing Gas Mask

iwojima4.jpg

U.S. Marines at Iwo Jima Beach

jima.jpg

U.S. Marines Raising Flag on Iwo Jima

injured2.jpg

U.S. Medics Helping Wounded Soldier

submarin.jpg

U.S. Naval Officer Using Submarine Periscope

sailor1.jpg

U.S. Navy Soldier

# Thumbnail Photo Images and Clip Art

soldiers.jpg

U.S. Soldiers on Battlefield

soldier2.jpg

U.S. Soldiers Storming North Africa Beach

grayback.jpg

U.S. Submarine Grayback

nautilus.jpg

U.S. Submarine Nautilus

miss4.jpg

U.S.S. Missouri 1

miss5.jpg

U.S.S. Missouri 2

miss3.jpg

U.S.S. Missouri & Blimp

miss6.jpg

U.S.S. Missouri Firing Guns at Night 1

miss7.jpg

U.S.S. Missouri Firing Guns at Night 2

miss2.jpg

U.S.S. Missouri Firing Guns 1

miss8.jpg

U.S.S. Missouri Firing Guns 2

injured.jpg

U.S. Wounded Soldier Being Transferred Between Ships

 

## Thumbnail Photo Images and Clip Art

uso3.jpg

USO & Donald Duck Poster

uso1.jpg

USO Poster

rooney.jpg

USO Show with Mickey Rooney

vjday1.jpg

V-J Day Parade in New York City

kissing.jpg

V-J Day Sailor Kissing Surprised Nurse

jeep1.jpg

War Bonds Pay for Jeep Parts Poster

bonds2.jpg

War Bonds Poster: Flag

bonds5.jpg

War Bonds Poster: Shadow of Swastika

bonds3.jpg

War Bonds Poster: Soldier & Girl

bonds6.jpg

War Bonds Poster: Uncle Sam

bonds4.jpg

War Bonds Poster: Woman & Children

bonds1.jpg

War Bonds Poster: Wounded Soldier

## Thumbnail Photo Images and Clip Art

church1.jpg

Winston Churchill

church2.jpg

Winston Churchill
Giving Radio Address

rosie3.jpg

Woman on Tractor

woman.jpg

Woman Operating
Machine

waac5.jpg

Woman Soldier
Operating Switchboard

rosie2.jpg

Woman Worker

rosie1.jpg

Women Factory
Workers 1

rosie5.jpg

Women Factory
Workers 2

rosie7.jpg

Women Factory
Workers 3

rosie8.jpg

Women Factory
Workers 4

w-unif.jpg

Women Soldiers at
Attention

waac3.jpg

Women Soldiers at Desk

 

# Thumbnail Photo Images and Clip Art

waac4.jpg

Women Soldiers Marching

rosie9.jpg

Women Workers Poster 1

rosie10.jpg

Women Workers Poster 2

waac1.jpg

Women's Army Corps Poster

waac2.jpg

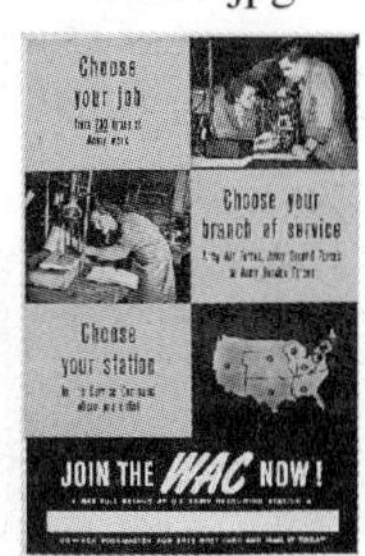



Women's Army Corps Recruitment Poster

# Audio Clips, Video Clips, and Documents

## Audio Clips

### Music

Song: "Any Bonds Today?"

### Sound Effects

Airplane 1
Airplane 2
Bomb
Ship Bell
Tank

### Speeches

Chamberlain Speech on German Aggression
Churchill's First Speech as Prime Minister
General MacArthur Accepts Japan's Surrender
Hitler Announcing Germany's Rearmament
Hoover Address at Onset of World War II in Europe
Iwo Jima Being Captured
Marshall Plan Speech
President Truman Announcing Victory over Germany
President Truman Announcing Victory over Japan
President Truman's Speech About Bombing Hiroshima
President Truman's Speech About the Atomic Bomb
Roosevelt's "Day of Infamy" Address
Roosevelt's Speech about the Four Freedoms
Winston Churchill's "This Was Their Finest Hour" Speech

## Video Clips

D-Day Invasion of Normandy
D-Day Invasion of Normandy (short movie)
General MacArthur Accepts Japan's Surrender
Hitler & Nazi Troops
Hitler Opening Olympic Games
Iwo Jima Being Captured
Pearl Harbor Attack
President Truman's Speech About Atomic Bomb

## Documents

Allies & Germany WWII Surrender Documents
Britain's Response to Germany's Invasion of Poland
Cairo Conference Declaration
France's Response to Germany's Invasion of Poland
Germany's Invasion of Poland
Japanese Attack on Pearl Harbor
Japanese Surrender Documents
Moscow Conference
Ogdensburg Agreement on Hemispheric Defense
Potsdam Proclamation
President Roosevelt's Radio Address
President Truman's Message to Congress About the Atomic Bomb
President Truman's Proclamation About President Roosevelt's Death
Soviet-Japanese Neutrality & Denunciation Pact
U.S. Congress Neutrality Act
U.S. Declaration of War on Germany
U.S. Declaration of War on Japan
U.S. Lend Lease Act
United Nations Charter
Yalta (Crimea) Conference